"The Spirit of VMI," renowned in deed and song, perhaps surpasses that of any other American college. That spirit is an intangible quality and defies definition. But it goes back through the years to the Battle of New Market and even before, and is part and parcel of the cadet corps. It perplexes an outsider. He can neither explain nor put his hand on it, but he's always aware of the "Spirit of VMI."

Chauncey Durden, *Richmond Times-Dispatch*, 1938

VIRGINIA

" — as a State institution, neither sectional nor denominational."

MILITARY

"— indicating its characteristic feature."

INSTITUTE

"— something different from either college or university."

VIRGINIA MILITARY INSTITUTE
The Spirit

PHOTOGRAPHED BY JIM RICHARDSON

HARMONY HOUSE
PUBLISHERS LOUISVILLE

VIRGINIA MILITARY INSTITUTE
1839 1989
OUR HERITAGE CONTINUES

Executive Editor: William Strode
Hardcover International Standard Book Number 0-916509-63-x
Library of Congress Catalog Number 89-080405
Printed in Canada
Color Separations by Four Colour Imports, Inc.
First printing Fall 1989 by Harmony House Publishers
Second printing fall 1994 by Harmony House Publishers
P. O. Box 90, Prospect, Kentucky 40059 (502) 228-4446
Copyright 1989 by Harmony House Publishers
Photographs copyright 1989 by Jim Richardson
Additional photographs pages 86-87 by Andres R. Alonso

Virginia Military Institute-The Spirit is an official commemorative project of the Virginia Military Institute
Sesquicentennial Committee. The Publisher acknowledges the special efforts of the book committee; Mr. Keith
Gibson, Colonel Tom Davis, Captain Diane Jacob, Mr. Tom Joynes, Mrs. Julie Martin and Mr. John Walters.
Special thanks are extended to Colonel David Harbach, VMI Commandant, and the VMI Corps of Cadets.

INTRODUCTION

"Virginia — a state institution, neither sectional nor denominational. Military — its characteristic feature. Institute — something different from either college or university. The three elements thus indicated are the basis of a triangular pyramid, of which the sides will preserve their mutual relation to whatever height the structure may rise."

In so explaining his choice of name for the new institution, John Thomas Lewis Preston, the young Lexington attorney generally credited with conceiving the idea of VMI, identified the features of the nation's first state military college—the first practical effort by a state to combine the work of a full college curriculum and the exacting daily regimen of military discipline. In the first twenty-five years, repeated testing forged a dedication to values—a sense of duty and honor—that have identified every generation of alumni since as VMI men.

For more than twenty years before the formation of the Institute in 1839, its site was occupied by a military post of the state of Virginia, serving as the storage point of arms for the western part of the Commonwealth. The arsenal guard, although living a strict military life while on duty, was lacking in self-discipline, and their leisure-time activities upset the quiet decorum of the valley community.

Plans for a change in the nature of the arsenal administration were discussed, and in 1834 the subject came into open debate among Lexington's leading citizens when it was proposed that the arsenal be transformed into a

A corner of a VMI barracks room, circa 1900

military college, with the students protecting the arms there while pursuing educational courses. The plan led to passage of legislation in the General Assembly establishing the Virginia Military Institute.

The State Engineer of Virginia, Colonel Claudius Crozet, a graduate of Ecole Polytechnique and former military officer under Napoleon, was elected to preside over the newly appointed Board of Visitors. Crozet's own experience as a cadet in France and as a professor of engineering at West Point prepared him well for the task ahead.

Today the Barracks, which still possesses much of the form and style envisioned by Davis and Smith more than 130 years ago, is widely recognized for its distinctive architecture. In 1966 it was designated a National Historic Landmark. Recent additions to the VMI campus continue to carry out the simplified Gothic lines of Davis's original designs. The striking sand-colored structures reflect the success with which Smith and Davis combined their talents to formulate "an adequate, tasteful design" and to provide for "the future extension of the buildings."

Royster Lyle, Jr., and Matthew Paxton, Jr., in *Virginia Cavalcade*, Winter 1974

In 1839, higher education was still in the classical mold. Men went to college to prepare for the ministry or law or medicine rather than for business or engineering. VMI was among the early leaders to break from tradition and provide scientific training for practical pursuits. A course in civil engineering has been conducted from the beginning. The first course in industrial chemistry in the South was offered here in 1846.

The Institute was a pioneer in another respect. Before the first class was graduated in 1842, VMI by legislative act began to serve as a college to provide efficient teachers for the schools of the Commonwealth. This service had far-reaching influence in building up the state's educational system.

Professor (later Major General) Francis H. Smith, a distinguished graduate of the United States Military Academy, was appointed Superintendent and presided over the affairs of the Institute for its first half-century. By 1850 the

Francis H. Smith, circa 1885

Corps was housed in a new barracks and other buildings were added. The curriculum was broadened and the faculty increased. Among

Cadets gathered at "Stonewall" Jackson's grave , circa 1868

the teachers in the early years was a moody, almost eccentric professor of natural philosophy—physics, as it is called today—named Thomas Jonathan Jackson, who joined the faculty in 1851 and served until April 1861, when he became one of the great commanders of American military history.

With the outbreak of the Civil War, the Cadet Corps was called under command of Jackson, who was to win fame as the immortal "Stonewall," to train recruits for the Confederate Army forming in Richmond. After serving as drill instructors for eight months, the Corps returned to the Institute in the interest of continuing its educational mission and the training of officers for the Southern armies. The Cadet Corps was called into active service a number of times in the Valley of Virginia during the next three years.

On May 15, 1863, the Corps of Cadets escorted the body of "Stonewall" Jackson to his grave in Lexington, following his death from wounds received at the battle of Chancellorsville. Just before the battle, Jackson, after surveying the field and seeing so many VMI

The role of the Corps at New Market, Virginia, on May 15, 1864, is a moment unique in American history. Each spring the Cadet Corps honors the ten from its ranks who died there; six are buried on the VMI grounds. In the fall, new cadets journey to the battlefield on which their predecessors proved their courage and the value of the VMI experience. New Market Battlefield Historical Park is a National Historic Landmark owned by VMI.

men around him in key positions, spoke the oft-quoted words: "The Institute will be heard from today."

One year to the day after the funeral of Jackson, the VMI Cadet Corps was engaged as a unit in pitched battle. Their service in the Battle of New Market has stood since as a

Ruins of barracks after Hunter's raid 1866

hallmark of the VMI heritage. The toll: ten cadets killed and 47 wounded. Six of the dead are buried at the site of the New Market monument on the VMI grounds.

The role of the Corps at New Market is a moment unique in American collegiate and military history. Just as unique is a trip taken every fall by entering cadets—Rats, as they are called—who journey to the battlefield on which their predecessors proved their courage and the value of the VMI educational experience. This citizen-soldier education assured that after the cessation of hostilities the New Market Corps was prepared for the careers and leadership roles so necessary to rebuilding their state and nation.

The Institute was shelled and burned on June 12, 1864, by Union forces under the command of General David Hunter. "I have grieved over the destruction of the Military In-

stitute," wrote General Robert E. Lee, "but the good that has been done to the country cannot be destroyed, nor can its name or fame perish. It will rise stronger than before and continue to diffuse its benefits to a grateful people." If it had not been for the courageous efforts of General Smith and the dedicated members of the faculty, it is doubtful that the Institute could have reopened in the war-ravaged South.

After 1865, buildings were replaced rapidly and the faculty grew in stature with the addition to the teaching staff of some of the most distinguished scientists in the country. Among them was Matthew Fontaine Maury, whose work in charting the ocean currents earned him the title of "The Pathfinder of the Seas." Both Jackson and Maury subsequently were elected to the Hall of Fame of Great Americans.

A century and a half after VMI began, the names of Smith, Preston, and Crozet linger, their example a model to the endless procession of young men who have been prepared by the

Commodore Matthew Fontaine Maury, circa 1864

Institute for the opportunities and obligations of citizenship. For today—and for tomorrow—it is an example nourished by a dedicated faculty and staff and the VMI Corps of Cadets.

South facade of barracks and cabins, circa 1875. Repairs made after Hunter's raid are visible in the contrast between the old and new mortar.

Engineering and drawing professor Robert A. Marr in his classroom, circa 1895.

Cadet room ready for inspection, circa 1930

Limit Gates, 1889. Thomas Hoomes Williamson, faculty member from 1841 to 1887, is generally credited with designing the Limit Gates.

Five veterans from the Battle of New Market, circa 1866-67. Clockwise from upper left: Cadets Hardaway H. Dinwiddie, Gaylord B. Clark, Thomas G. Hayes, John L. Tunstall, and Edward M. Tutwiler. All were members of the Class of 1867.

The Corps marching in William Howard Taft's inaugural parade, March 4, 1909.

"Class Parade" - marching through barracks courtyard, circa 1904.

A different use for the parade ground — an airplane lands on the parade ground, circa 1920, as a crowd in front of barracks observes. The 1907 library is seen in the background on left.

Final Ball 1918, Jackson Memorial Hall gymnasium.

Classroom scene, 1899.

1836	First Act of Virginia legislature to organize military school at Lexington Arsenal.
1837	Claudius Crozet appointed president of first Board of Visitors; serves until 1845.
1839	Institute opens November 11 with Francis Henney Smith as principal professor, 25 cadets enrolled.
1841	Smith is designated superintendent; faculty expanded to three.
1842	First cadets become graduates and create the Alumni Association.
1845	Four-year program established. Addition of B Company introduces term Cadet Battalion.
1846	First graduates enter military service during Mexican War.
1849	Architect A. J. Davis develops building plan in Gothic style.
1851	Barracks completed; Jackson becomes professor of natural and experimental philosophy.
1861	Civil War begins. Corps ordered to Richmond, serving from April to December.
1862	Cadets in service at McDowell Campaign.
1863	Jackson dies at Chancellorsville and is buried in Lexington.
1864	Corps at Battle of New Market: 10 dead, 47 wounded. VMI shelled and burned by forces of Union General David Hunter. Corps relocated to Richmond Alms House.
1865	Corps serves in defense of Richmond until war ends in April. VMI reopens in makeshift quarters in the fall.
1868	Reconstruction completed on barracks, mess hall, and other buildings. Military arms restored to the Corps, whose strength reaches 260. Commodore Matthew Fontaine Maury joins faculty.
1885	VMI *BOMB* becomes first college yearbook in the South.
1889	Major General Francis H. Smith, builder and rebuilder of VMI, retires after 50 years.
1890	Brigadier General Scott Shipp, VMI 1859, becomes second superintendent.
1891	VMI wins its first football game.
1907	Major General Edward West Nichols, VMI 1878, becomes third superintendent.
1912	Bachelor of Science degree awarded to all graduates; Jackson statue erected.
1915	Bachelor of Arts degree offered in liberal arts. Jackson Memorial Hall erected with federal funds provided by U. S. Congress in restitution for Civil War damages.
1916	Benjamin Bowering, VMI 1915, composes *The VMI Spirit.*
1918	During World War I more than 2,000 VMI men serve in National Defense roles.
1919	Army ROTC formally established at VMI; 100 horses arrive for mounted drill.
1920	Flying Squadron gives VMI its first undefeated football season.
1921	First reserve commissions awarded at graduation. First Rhodes Scholar named at VMI.
1923	VMI joins Southern Conference.

HISTORICAL DATES OF VMI

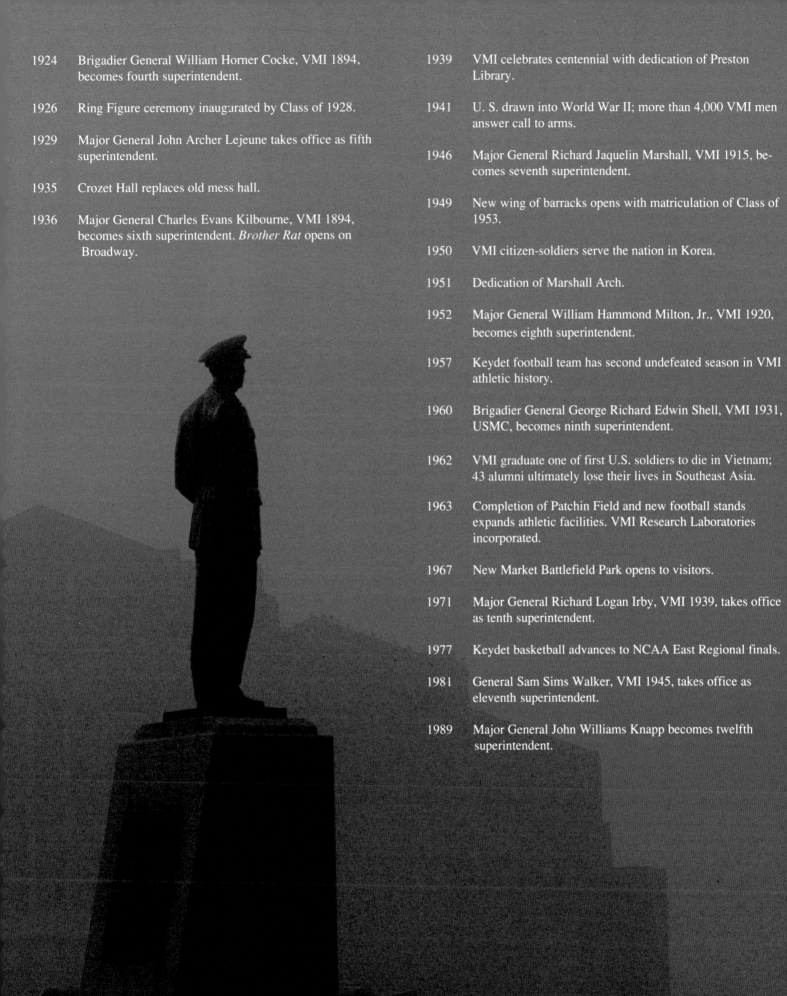

1924	Brigadier General William Horner Cocke, VMI 1894, becomes fourth superintendent.
1926	Ring Figure ceremony inaugurated by Class of 1928.
1929	Major General John Archer Lejeune takes office as fifth superintendent.
1935	Crozet Hall replaces old mess hall.
1936	Major General Charles Evans Kilbourne, VMI 1894, becomes sixth superintendent. *Brother Rat* opens on Broadway.
1939	VMI celebrates centennial with dedication of Preston Library.
1941	U. S. drawn into World War II; more than 4,000 VMI men answer call to arms.
1946	Major General Richard Jaquelin Marshall, VMI 1915, becomes seventh superintendent.
1949	New wing of barracks opens with matriculation of Class of 1953.
1950	VMI citizen-soldiers serve the nation in Korea.
1951	Dedication of Marshall Arch.
1952	Major General William Hammond Milton, Jr., VMI 1920, becomes eighth superintendent.
1957	Keydet football team has second undefeated season in VMI athletic history.
1960	Brigadier General George Richard Edwin Shell, VMI 1931, USMC, becomes ninth superintendent.
1962	VMI graduate one of first U.S. soldiers to die in Vietnam; 43 alumni ultimately lose their lives in Southeast Asia.
1963	Completion of Patchin Field and new football stands expands athletic facilities. VMI Research Laboratories incorporated.
1967	New Market Battlefield Park opens to visitors.
1971	Major General Richard Logan Irby, VMI 1939, takes office as tenth superintendent.
1977	Keydet basketball advances to NCAA East Regional finals.
1981	General Sam Sims Walker, VMI 1945, takes office as eleventh superintendent.
1989	Major General John Williams Knapp becomes twelfth superintendent.

The sons of VMI can lay down their ploughs and their pens tonight and pick up their swords and rifles tomorrow;
they can step from office or warehouse or store into marching regiment and immediately catch step; for, in obtaining
an education which fits them for civil life, they have acquired also the education which makes them invaluable in the
defense of their country when that country has to go outside its professional men of arms and call upon the citizen to
exercise what is at once his privilege and his duty of defending his native land.

THE HEALTHFVL AND PLEASANT
YOVTHS PRESSING VP THE HILL
A GRATIFYING SPECTACLE AN
STATE OBJECTS OF HONEST PRI
SPECIMENS OF CITIZEN SOLDIER
PROVD OF HER FAME AND READ
TO VINDICATE HER HON

COL J

... OF A CROWD OF HONORABLE
... NCE WITH NOBLE EMVLATION
... TO OVR COVNTRY AND OVR
... THEIR INSTRVCTORS AND FAIR
... ACHED TO THEIR NATIVE STATE
... EVERY TIME OF DEEPEST PERIL
... R DEFEND HER RIGHTS
... LESTON

The Institute gave me not only a standard of my daily conduct among men, but it endowed me with a heritage of honor and self-sacrifice.

General George C. Marshall, '01, Commencement address, June 1940

YOU MAY BE WHATEVER YOU RESOLVE

"STONEWAL

A ny school that can boast of graduates like General Marshall — and all his associates who have been so valuable in wartime and peacetime service to this country — is indeed a distinguished institution and one that we certainly will nourish as long as there is an America.

President Dwight D. Eisenhower, 1958

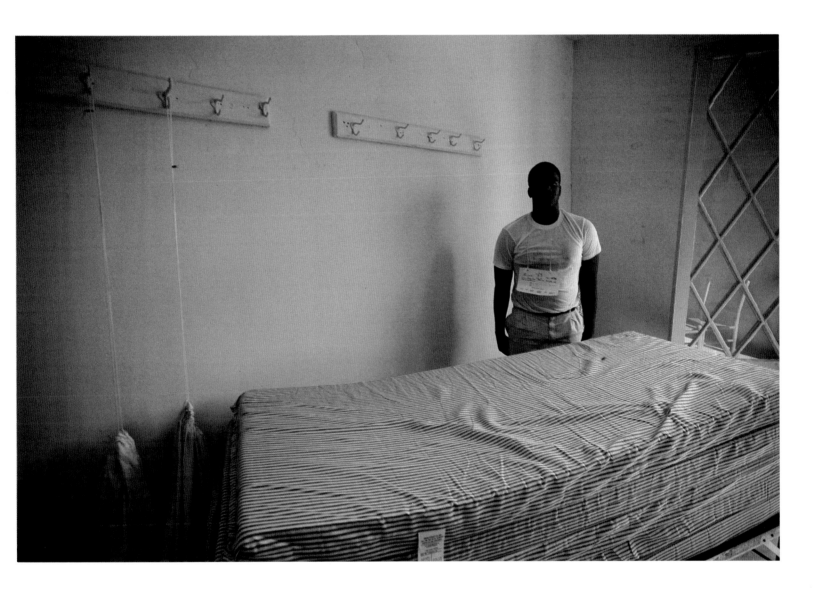

I*t matters not under what adventitious circumstances you may have come here — of wealth, or family, or association — every prop is now wrested from you but that which supports your own merits — your personal, individual action and desert . . . The system of government in this institution happily conspires to help you in this work, not by diminishing your responsibility, but by defining and enforcing it.*

From *The Inner Life of the VMI Cadet*, an address to the Corps by Francis H. Smith, Superintendent, September 10, 1866

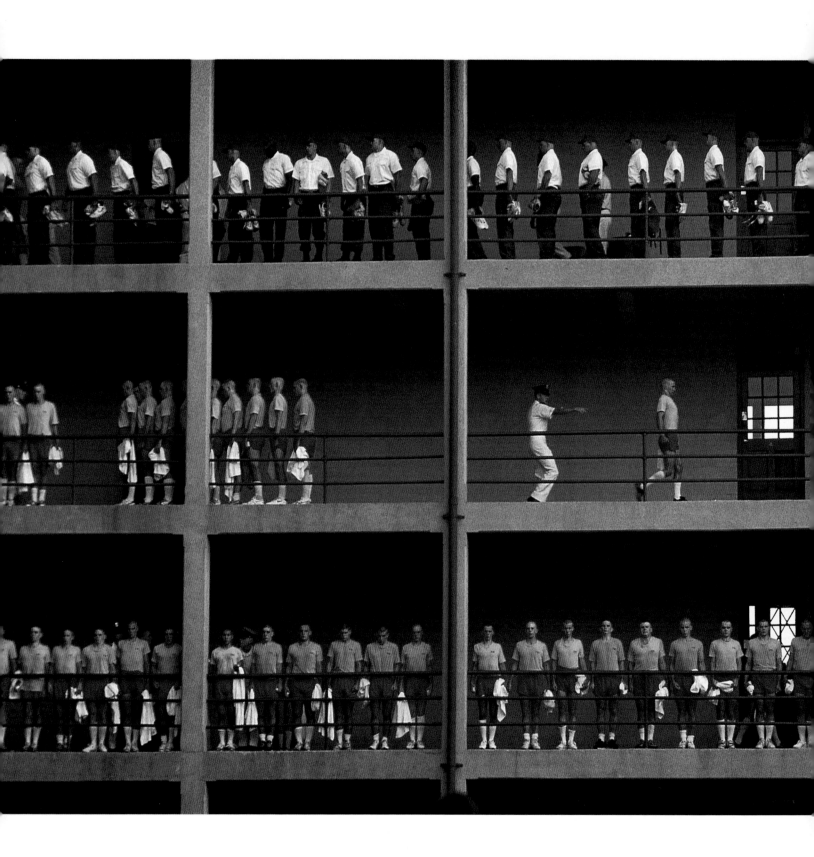

L*ife at VMI . . . nothing like anything one has ever experienced before, neither is it something one will experience again . . . It is a life characterized by former cadets as one they would not take a million dollars for having lived, and wouldn't take a million dollars to go through again.*

Henry A. Wise, '27, *Drawing Out the Man: The VMI Story*, 1978

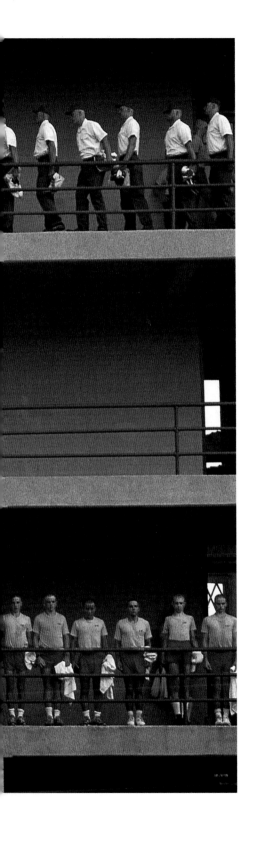

F*rom the first day as a Rat to that proud day when we receive a VMI diploma we are taught that honesty, self-discipline, teamwork, sensitivity to others, personal acceptance of responsibility and accountability, individual effort, courage and the brotherhood of man are the foundation stones of a successful democratic society. Yes, we VMI men are fortunate to have experienced such basics of citizenship . . . But, VMI can only provide the beginning — it is up to us to run the race. It is the degree to which we as individuals practice those principles as we go through life that the malaise affecting our country will be cured, that our place in society will be determined and the place of our total society in the whole world will be determined.*

John D. deButts, '36, Chairman of the Board, AT & T, November 11, 1975

51

It has always been a place of extraordinary loneliness — of symbolic, traditional, awe inspiring silence.

Age shows; it is pervasive; it exudes and hangs heavy as a vapor. The Institute is a cold place, yet paradoxically emits a hidden warmth.

The cinereous coolness often seems to dominate, to engulf the soul; it appears to be every-where — in the sky, on the walls, on the grounds, on the trees — and even in the faces. There are many lonelinesses: one overwhelms, like the weight of towering and aloof walls that loom on every side; another manifests itself in the ultimate realization that the whole responsibility of succeeding, excelling . . . finally rests with you alone.

From *The Bomb*, 1970

George C. Marshall Research Library and Museum

The psychology of the new cadets is interesting . . . The first two or three months they think and say that the Institute next to the Infernal Regions is the worst, the very worst place of which they have ever heard; during the next two or three months they say that their experiences have not been bad at all; and then as they approach the end of their first year they will take pride in the fact that they have stood 'the gaff' and that they would not take the world for their experiences.

Lieutenant General Edward West Nichols, Superintendent, 1907-1924

In honoring VMI, you really honor its product . . . namely, a body of men trained to leave careers of their own choosing to serve as citizen-soldiers in time of national peril — educated men of discipline and honor, who, for nearly 150 years, have gone forth from VMI to assume leadership positions in all aspects of our national life.

Senator Harry F. Byrd, Jr., '35, address at the Virginia Meeting of the Newcomen Society of the United States, March 26, 1984

*V*MI builds what the nation needs. VMI builds that without
which the nation cannot endure. VMI is the builder of men.

Governor J. Lindsay Almond, Jr., December 12, 1959

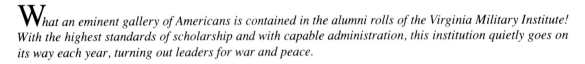

*W*hat *an eminent gallery of Americans is contained in the alumni rolls of the Virginia Military Institute! With the highest standards of scholarship and with capable administration, this institution quietly goes on its way each year, turning out leaders for war and peace.*

Richmond News Leader, February 10, 1956

69

O*f all the state's schools and colleges, the one most productive of genius per student and per tax dollar is the amazing little Virginia Military Institute.*

Benjamin Muse, *The Washington Post*, September 18, 1949

T*his country should never get so wrapped up in technology and the miracle of missiles to forget the continuing and greater requirement for our youth and manpower to speak up and stand up for service and duty — and here's where VMI excels.*

Carter L. Burgess, '39, Chairman of the Board, AMF, Founders Day address, November 11, 1966

H*ere is at least one institution that holds fast to values proved sound over five generations. Refusal to throw out what is demonstrably good simply in favor of novelty or caprice has led some, who disdain the meaning of education in its historic sense, to dub VMI an anachronism. If that word means that the school serves no cogent purpose or is moribund, the characterization is wrong. Growth in the academic area, in physical plant, in almost every facet has been admirable, especially considering the obstacles. Yet nowhere is more apt the phrase "The more things change, the more they remain the same."*

Henry A. Wise, '27, in *Drawing Out the Man: The VMI Story*, 1978

Jackson Memorial Hall

To every VMI man who ponders the significance of the day we are here to observe, there must inevitably come the question, Why. Why, each year do we make a point of remembering a battle which, after all, is only a footnote in the vast saga of the Civil War, particularly now when even that historic event is receding steadily into the remote and dusty past? . . .

We remember the New Market cadets because they represent both a challenge and a support. I believe that the VMI Spirit was born on that May day in 1864, and I believe that the New Market Corps stands as a bond among all who have worn the cadet gray. Every cadet, every alumnus, is forever able to draw upon one stirring and reassuring thought, the thought that if they could do it, so, God willing, can I.

Chester B. Goolrick, Jr., VMI '37

A *reputation is an achievement of yesterday — to be lived today and guarded tomorrow . . . With such a military and civic record before you, you cannot, you dare not, you will not fail when your opportunity comes. Because you too have lived the life of a VMI cadet . . .*

Colonel William Couper, '04, in *One Hundred Years at VMI,* 1939

Scarcely 25 years old, VMI was such a valued source of officers that Confederate leaders were loath to risk losing its cadets in combat; their primary contribution had been to drill green troops at Richmond. One 33-year-old recruit later reflected on his boyish VMI instructor: "How I hated that little cadet! He was always so wide-awake, so clean, so interested in the drill."

From *The Shenandoah in Flames*, by Thomas A. Lewis, Time-Life Books, 1987

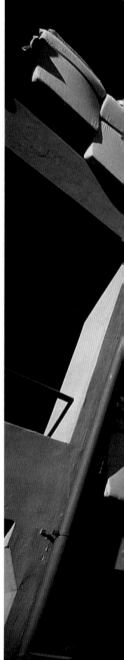

There is no school anywhere remotely like the Virginia Military Institute. It is a special place, with battlements mustard-colored in the setting sun, on a bluff above the Maury River, within sight of Virginia's Blue Ridge Mountains. Its athletic teams perform prodigies of valor out of all proportion to the student body of 1,300. A military maxim says that morale is to physical as three to one, and opponents of VMI have an uneasy sense, when they take the field, that whatever the betting odds may be in a game, the 3-to-1 ratio for morale always attends the Flying Squadron.

Guy Friddell in the Foreword to *The Corps Roots the Loudest* by Thomas W. Davis, '64

*V*ictory is no great matter, and defeat is even less; the essential thing in good sport is the manly striving to excel, and the good feeling it fosters between those who play fair and have no excuses when they lose.

Constitution and By-Laws of the VMI Athletic Association, 1917

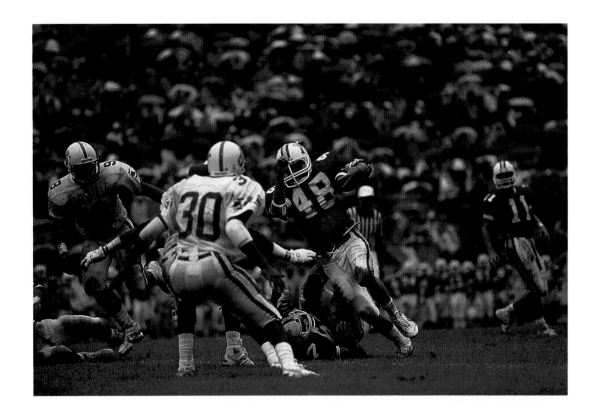

The often misused adjective 'unique' does not seem out of place in describing VMI's present position within the educational framework of Virginia, and, indeed, within the national collegiate spectrum. It was the first state-supported military college, and it is today the last of the country's classic military colleges, in that every student is required to take rigorous military training within the Spartan VMI barracks as part of a program that, however, places first emphasis on academics. At a time when cynicism, permissiveness, and lax standards are far too prevalent, VMI still adheres to education for the whole man: high academic standards, military discipline, physical fitness and a high moral character. VMI has a student-administered honor code of a genre with next-door Washington and Lee University's in insisting that gentlemen do not lie, cheat, or steal.

The VMI approach is not for everyone, to be sure. But all Virginians benefit immensely by having a VMI within the wide range of collegiate choice offered in this state.

Editorial, *Richmond Times-Dispatch*, November 4, 1979

Bas-relief bronze of General Lemuel C. Shepherd, Jr., VMI 1917, Commandant of the Marine Corps, 1952-1956

There *is a spirit that radiates from the Virginia Military Institute and permeates every man who has ever graduated here. It is a spirit proved time and time again in the defense of this nation and of this state and is reflected in the illustrious names of history that have so often been associated with this institution.*

Governor Mills E. Godwin, Jr., Commencement address, 1966

P*robably no fraternity in our scholastic world is closer than that of the graduates
and cadets of the Virginia Military Institute.*

The Morning Tribune, New Orleans

T*here is no firmer bond than that which holds the graduates of VMI together . . . There is an essence here that permeates deep into the consciousness of all of you, that leaves its mark in every graduate of VMI. And I know of no finer distinction that could be had anywhere.*

Governor Mills E. Godwin, Jr., Founders Day address, November 11, 1975

In the way you regard the Institute you are at this time like visitors to a great museum or gallery of art. You are standing very close to a huge canvas: so close you can see the fissures and cracks, the bright and fading pigments, the lapidary varnish, the dust. Some of you have already stepped back from the canvas and seen the majesty of the artist's conception and design; many of you have not; but all of you will. You will find then the painting majestic, proud, wonderfully-proportioned; and the impression it will leave upon your minds and characters will be the most profound of your lives.

Josiah Bunting, III, '63, President, Briarcliff College, Commencement address, 1974

Whatever we do it will be as men of VMI.

John D. deButts, '36